ISABELLE BOILY

Achieving Financial Freedom: How to make money work for you

Embark on a transformative journey towards financial abundance and unlock the secrets to making money work for you.

First edition

This book was professionally typeset on Reedsy.
Find out more at reedsy.com

Contents

1

Introduction

The Journey Begins

Welcome to your financial independence. My name is Isabelle Boily, and I am very excited to finally put into words everything that has been on my mind for far too long. As the founder of Success Elevator, where I help people achieve soaring success by effectively removing lifelong blocks and limitations, it was inevitable that I would eventually create a series of books and guides to provide people with quick references on various topics related to success. Now, I am not talking about the infamous shallow success, but rather all the small life steps and actions that lead you to a life goal or the realization of a dream.

Let's get back to the main subject: financial freedom and making money work for you. Aren't we all living to meet the end of the month and being able to offer ourselves some yearly family vacation, a new car, dinner at the restaurant, paying for our kids' school tuition, clothes, etc.?

Sadly, 40% of Americans are struggling to pay their monthly bills. This is already way too much, and with the unstable economics everywhere, it looks like these numbers will just keep increasing.

The good news is that everything is there and available for us. All we have to do is be aware of it, prepare ourselves to take action, and grab the opportunity.

Financial freedom holds immense importance for each one of us and our families due to its profound impact on various aspects of life. Don't get me wrong here; it is not just about accumulating wealth; it's about gaining control over one's financial destiny and using that control to live a fulfilling and purposeful life. It also provides the means to pursue dreams, make choices aligned with personal values, and contribute positively to one's own life and the lives of others. It empowers individuals to rely on their own resources, significantly reduces dependency on external resources, and adds flexibility and independence. It also gives us freedom of choice in how we spend our time.

Financial freedom contributes to an improved quality of life, giving us access to better healthcare, education, housing, and overall well-being. And if we transfer that to entrepreneurship, it gives us the cash flow to start our own business, contributing to economic growth. What about personal growth and development? It is an important part of our thriving journey.

I could go on for hours, but let's just say that, above all, it gives us a sense of security and peace of mind.

This book might challenge some of your deeply anchored beliefs; please take it with an open mind. What we open ourselves to is creating new thoughts, expanding our minds, and attracting new opportunities in our lives. You might not agree with everything that is coming, and that is totally fine. This book is also a reference; if there is a part you know already or don't adhere to, simply skip it. Although I would love for you to read it fully, I will respect your choice.

I hope you will find new insights and useful information that will lead you to take action and move towards a life where financial and time freedom will be part of it. You deserve it; it is your birthright.

Let's dive in and create new opportunities.

2

Defining Financial Freedom

What does financial freedom mean?

Financial freedom is not merely a destination; it's a transformative journey that empowers individuals to take control of their economic well-being and live life on their terms. Financial freedom is fundamentally the capacity to make decisions free from financial constraints. It goes beyond the traditional notion of wealth and consists of the freedom to pursue passions, make meaningful life choices, and create a future of abundance.

Imagine waking up each day with the peace of mind that your financial foundation is solid and that you have the flexibility to design your life as you see fit. Financial freedom is about breaking free from the shackles of financial stress, allowing you to focus on what truly matters. It is the liberation from the paycheck-to-paycheck cycle, the elimination of debt-induced anxieties, and the empowerment to make decisions based on your aspirations rather than financial constraints.

Achieving financial freedom involves mastering the art of budgeting, investing wisely, and cultivating a mindset of abundance. It's a dynamic process that requires discipline, strategic planning, and a commitment to continuous learning. Financial freedom is not a one-size-fits-all concept; it's about defining what it means for you personally and aligning your actions with those aspirations.

Moreover, financial freedom extends beyond individual prosperity; it creates a ripple effect in communities. When individuals achieve financial freedom, they are better positioned to contribute positively to society, whether through philanthropy, mentorship, or supporting local businesses.

Basically, financial freedom is the gateway to a life where worries about bills, unexpected expenses, or financial limitations no longer dictate your choices. It's a journey of empowerment, self-discovery, and the pursuit of a life rich in both financial and personal fulfillment. As you begin this journey, keep in mind that the goal is not only financial independence but also the freedom to live your life on your own terms and make a lasting impact.

Setting personalized financial goals

Setting personalized financial goals is a crucial step toward achieving financial independence. Imagine these goals as your compass, guiding you through the twists and turns of your financial situation. They aren't just numbers; they're the stepping stones to the life you envision.

Begin with introspection. What does financial freedom look like for you? Is it owning a home, traveling the world, or retiring early? Your goals should echo your dreams and reflect your values. Be specific; define not just what you want but when you want it. This clarity transforms vague aspirations into tangible targets.

Consider short-term and long-term objectives. Short-term goals create a sense of accomplishment and momentum, like building an emergency fund. Long-term goals, such as retirement or a child's education, require strategic planning and consistent effort.

Break down these goals into bite-sized tasks. If saving for a home, outline steps like researching mortgage options or cutting unnecessary expenses. This not only simplifies the journey but also allows you to celebrate smaller victories along the way.

Flexibility is key. Life is dynamic, and so should be your goals. Regularly review and adjust them as circumstances evolve. This doesn't signal failure; it's a testament to adaptability and growth.

Track your progress diligently. Create a visual representation, a vision board, or a financial tracker to stay motivated. Celebrate milestones, learn from setbacks, and stay committed to the bigger picture.

Remember, these goals are not restrictions but liberators. They provide direction without stifling spontaneity. Setting personalized financial goals is not just about amassing wealth; it's about sculpting a life aligned with your values and aspirations. It's about having the financial means to say 'yes' to opportunities that resonate with your soul.

So, dream big, set those goals, and let them propel you towards a future where financial independence is not just a destination but a way of life. You've got this. Let's embark on this transformative journey together.

3

Mindset vs. Action

O f course, I could not write a book without emphasizing the importance of mindset. After all, it is my passion and my area of expertise!

It's truly remarkable how much our thoughts, beliefs, and the words we speak to ourselves can shape our behaviors and ultimately determine our outcomes. It's important to recognize the immense impact they have on our lives. They are the foundation of our reality, shaping everything around us. Creating a mindset that is focused on growth and positivity is the key to propelling us forward. It's truly empowering to embrace self-reflection, analyze the stories we tell ourselves, and reshape our internal dialogue to align with our goals.

The power of The 80% Mindset, 20% Action Principle

When it comes to personal and professional achievement, the 80% mindset, 20% action approach truly embodies wisdom and serves as an inspiring example. This idea highlights the power of our mindset in achieving success, with our physical efforts playing a supporting role. It emphasizes the importance of our mental approach to accomplishing great things.

This principle challenges the conventional belief that success is solely achieved through constant action, highlighting the significance of thoughtful consideration in guiding us towards our goals. Having the right mindset is crucial, accounting for a significant 80% of the work.

It's incredible how those who consistently take massive action are bound to achieve their desired results, even if it may take a bit longer. Embrace the incredible power of your mind, which has the ability to guide you towards your desired destination.

Take advantage of this amazing tool that resides within each and every one of us. Let's focus on setting clear intentions and envisioning the results we want to achieve. By being open and ready to receive, we can make it happen. Having the appropriate mindset is also essential to success, but it's equally important to take action. Just visualizing and manifesting alone won't get you very far unless you pair it with some action.

The 20% action component is crucial for achieving our goals. It encompasses the practical steps, decisions, and efforts that we must take to make our dreams a reality. When you combine strategic action with a strong mindset, the results become incredibly powerful. It's amazing how much you can achieve when you approach things with determination and focus. Keep pushing forward and watch how your efforts pay off! It involves taking intentional, goal-oriented actions that align with the vision we've set, amplifying the impact of our endeavors.

Overcoming common mental barriers to financial freedom

Embarking on the road to financial freedom is a phenomenal experience that goes beyond just crunching numbers. It's a psychological adventure where we conquer common mental barriers to unlock the path to prosperity. One common challenge that many people face is the fear of scarcity, where they constantly believe that there is never enough. Take on an abundance mindset to challenge this notion. Adopt a positive mindset by acknowledging and appreciating your present financial successes, regardless of their size.

Another hurdle to overcome is the fear of failure. Always remember that setbacks are simply stepping stones on your journey, not roadblocks. Keep pushing forward and never lose sight of your goals. Embrace the lessons from financial missteps, make necessary adjustments, and keep pushing forward. Achieving financial freedom requires ongoing devotion and unwavering determination. Your ability to bounce back from setbacks is crucial on this journey.

Procrastination can be quite a challenge to overcome. Don't underestimate the power of taking action when it comes to your finances. Every moment counts, and each decision you make has the potential to create positive outcomes. Embrace the opportunities that lie ahead and seize them with enthusiasm. By breaking down tasks into smaller, more manageable steps, you can create a sense of accomplishment along the way. This approach allows you to tackle each step with enthusiasm and motivation, knowing that you are making progress towards your goal.

Keep pushing forward and celebrating each milestone you reach! The power of compounding extends far beyond investments; it has an equally profound impact on overcoming financial inertia.

Embrace the uniqueness of each individual. Every financial journey is distinctive and shaped by individual circumstances. Instead of comparing yourself to others, keep your focus on your goals, values, and the progress you've already made. Keep pushing forward! Every individual's journey to financial freedom is as unique as their own fingerprint.

Recognizing the importance of knowing your finances is absolutely crucial. Having a solid understanding can help alleviate anxiety. Take the initiative to educate yourself about investments, budgeting, and financial planning. It's a valuable step towards building a brighter financial future. Knowledge is not only powerful, but it also serves as a potent antidote to uncertainty.

Finally, it's important to acknowledge and confront any negative beliefs you may have about money. Our upbringing and societal influence can sometimes hold us back from achieving financial growth. Replace them with beliefs that inspire and align with your aspirations.

When striving for financial freedom, the mind becomes the battle-ground. As you navigate these mental barriers, keep in mind that this journey is not only about accumulating wealth but also about discovering yourself. You have what it takes to overcome these challenges.

Stay positive and keep pushing forward. You've got this! By confronting these mental barriers directly, you are not only ensuring a secure financial future but also unlocking your potential for a life filled with abundance and fulfillment. Together, we can overcome any obstacles and cultivate a mindset that will propel you towards achieving lasting financial freedom.

.

4

Making Money Online

The concepts of making money online and the "work from anywhere" lifestyle

Welcome to the era of making money online and embracing the "work from anywhere" lifestyle. Picture this: your office is wherever you choose it to be, whether it's a beachside paradise, a cozy cafe, or the comfort of your own home. It's more than just a dream; it's a tangible reality that is transforming the way we work and live.

The concept of making money online has shattered traditional work boundaries. The digital landscape is filled with countless opportunities, ranging from freelancing gigs to creating online businesses. The possibilities are limitless! It's about combining your skills, passions, and expertise to create a career that matches your life goals.

Embracing the "work from anywhere" lifestyle is not just about the location; it's a mindset. It's the freedom to design your day, prioritize what matters most, and break free from the 9-to-5 shackles. Technology has transformed our work culture, allowing us to connect, collaborate, and contribute from virtually any corner of the globe.

However, success in the online arena requires a blend of entrepreneurial spirit, adaptability, and a strategic approach. No matter what your interests are, whether it's e-commerce, digital marketing, or content creation, it's essential to stay updated on market trends and consistently improve your skills. Keep pushing forward, and never stop learning!

Discovering the perfect balance between your passion and the needs of the market is the key to conquering this digital frontier. What do you love doing that others find valuable? That's your golden ticket. From affiliate marketing to online courses, the online world is a playground full of possibilities waiting to be discovered.

However, in order to fully embrace the benefits of flexibility, it is important that you maintain a sense of discipline and structure. The "work from anywhere" lifestyle thrives on balance. Set clear boundaries, establish a routine, and savor the freedom without compromising productivity.

Are you prepared to break free from the limitations of a traditional workplace?

The digital landscape is filled with countless opportunities for online income, waiting to be explored and embraced. Explore a wide range of opportunities, from freelancing and affiliate marketing to e-commerce and online courses. The options are diverse and cater to your unique interests and skills.

Imagine a world where your love for photography blossoms into a successful freelance venture or where your expertise becomes a profitable online course. Welcome to the digital space, a vibrant marketplace where creativity and commerce converge. Here, your unique offerings have the opportunity to reach a global audience, allowing you to showcase your talents and ideas to the world.

One great example is affiliate marketing, which gives you the opportunity to earn commissions by promoting products or services. By becoming an affiliate, you have the opportunity to become a digital influencer, sharing your genuine recommendations for products and earning a portion of the profits. On the other hand, e-commerce provides a wonderful opportunity to sell products worldwide, whether they are unique handmade crafts or cutting-edge gadgets.

The online world has truly revolutionized entrepreneurship, empowering individuals to share their talents and creations with a wide and interconnected audience. It's incredible how this platform has opened up endless possibilities for people to showcase their skills and pursue their passions. It's a testament to the power of technology and the positive impact it can have on our lives.

Strategies for Starting and Scaling Online Ventures:

Launching an online business requires a well-planned and methodical approach. Start by finding your niche. What makes you unique in the digital marketplace? Whether you are offering a service, selling products, or sharing knowledge, it is important to understand your unique value proposition. This clarity will help you stand out and attract customers, making your business more successful. Use digital platforms like social media, websites, and online marketplaces to establish a strong presence and connect with potential customers.

Expanding your online venture requires a blend of creativity, adaptability, and impactful promotion. Take the time to truly understand your target audience and fine-tune your offerings to meet their needs. Harness the power of digital marketing tools like social media advertising and search engine optimization to broaden your reach and captivate a wider audience.

Automation has revolutionized the online world, bringing about significant changes. By utilizing tools and systems to streamline processes, you can effectively scale your operations. By using automation, you can streamline tasks like email campaigns, customer relationship management, and e-commerce transactions. This not only saves you time but also allows you to focus on strategic planning and expanding your business.

Having a mindset of continuous learning is absolutely crucial in today's rapidly evolving digital landscape. Keep up with the latest industry trends, emerging technologies, and evolving consumer preferences. Use the opportunities provided by online courses, webinars, and networking events to continuously enhance your skillset and maintain a competitive edge in your field.

The digital landscape provides an incredible platform for individuals to pursue their passions and share their unique voice and offerings. Whether you're embarking on a freelance business, launching an e-commerce store, or creating online courses, the possibilities for success and growth are endless.

If you are in need of inspiration, the case studies and success stories of online entrepreneurs are truly uplifting. They showcase the incredible achievements and triumphs of individuals who have found success in the online world.

These stories serve as a source of motivation, reminding us of the limitless opportunities and potential that exist in the world of online business. These individuals showcase the wide range of paths to success in the online world, from graphic designers to e-commerce enthusiasts and course creators.

Their journeys demonstrate the ease of entrepreneurship in the digital age, where enthusiasm, commitment, and a strategic mindset lead to success online. Research them in your niche, follow them on their social media, and read their book; they already pave the road and will lead you to your own success.

Your creative touch has the potential to open up countless opportunities that are just waiting to be discovered. Know that the challenges that come your way are stepping stones towards your success, and with determination and a positive mindset, you have the power to achieve great things.

5

The Essential Tools and Platforms for Launching Your Remote Career

More and more traditional companies are recognizing the benefits of remote work, which is creating exciting new possibilities across different industries. There are numerous remote job opportunities available, spanning fields such as marketing, customer service, programming, and project management. Job platforms like **Remote OK, FlexJobs,** and **We Work Remotely** are incredible resources for discovering remote positions.

Freelancing has become incredibly accessible with platforms like **Upwork, Fiverr,** and **Freelancer**. These platforms provide individuals with the opportunity to showcase their skills and services to a global market, opening up a world of possibilities. No matter what your profession is, freelancing offers you the freedom to select your own projects and clients. It's a great way to have control over your work and enjoy the flexibility it brings.

Freelancing opens up a world of possibilities for individuals with specialized skills. It provides a platform for them to showcase their talents and explore new horizons. The platforms mentioned above provide a great opportunity for graphic designers, writers, program-mers, and consultants to showcase their expertise. Businesses actively seek freelance talent for short-term projects, making it a positive and motivating environment for professionals to demonstrate their skills. The flexibility allows for a wide range of work and clients, creating a diverse portfolio.

Digital nomads often gravitate towards careers in content creation, blogging, affiliate marketing, and e-commerce. These fields offer exciting opportunities for remote work and can provide a sense of fulfillment and freedom. Many individuals find joy and success in pursuing these paths, as they allow for creative expression and the ability to work from anywhere in the world. Adopting these career paths can lead to a fulfilling and rewarding lifestyle as a digital nomad. Platforms such as **Nomad List** and **Remote Year** are dedicated to serving this vibrant community, providing valuable information about destinations that are perfect for digital nomads.

Remote work opportunities have opened up new possibilities for professionals, allowing them to work from any location with flexibility. Companies recognize the importance of talent and prioritize it over geographical boundaries, creating a diverse and global workforce. We have a variety of roles available, including customer support, software development, marketing, and project management. Platforms such as **LinkedIn, Indeed,** and **Glassdoor** offer a wide range of remote job listings across various industries.

Adopting a location-independent lifestyle, digital nomads redefine the traditional nine-to-five grind. Content creators, travel bloggers, affiliate marketers, and e-commerce entrepreneurs utilize their skills to maintain a nomadic lifestyle. Social media platforms, personal blogs, and e-commerce websites provide opportunities for individuals and businesses to establish and promote their brand.

Upwork is the ultimate platform that effortlessly connects clients with freelance professionals. Craft a compelling profile that showcases your unique skills and expertise, allowing you to confidently bid on projects spanning a wide range of categories.

FlexJobs is your go-to platform for finding remote and flexible positions. Discover a wide range of exciting opportunities tailored to fit your unique needs, whether it's flexible work arrangements or diverse industries.

Nomad List is a platform that draws on the wisdom of a thriving community. Discover invaluable insights into the top destinations for digital nomads, empowering you to make informed choices for your next adventure. Find vibrant cities that offer a range of benefits, such as affordable living, fast internet connections, and a strong sense of community.

Remote OK is a popular board for remote positions. Explore a diverse selection of remote job opportunities available from companies across the globe.

We Work Remotely is the ultimate platform for finding remote job opportunities in a wide range of industries. We are dedicated to connecting talented individuals like you with positive and fulfilling work experiences. Whether you're a seasoned professional or just starting out, our platform is designed to help you find the perfect remote job that suits your skills and interests. Discover a wide range of remote opportunities, including full-time, part-time, and freelance positions.

Remote Year is an incredible program designed specifically for digital nomads like you. It provides a unique opportunity to embark on curated travel experiences that will undoubtedly enrich your life. You can explore new destinations while maintaining a positive and motivated mindset. It's the perfect way to enhance your fluency in different cultures and languages. Experience the incredible opportunity to connect with a vibrant community of individuals who share your passion, all while enjoying the freedom of remote work from anywhere in the world.

.

6

Equipping Yourself for Success

Equipping Yourself for Success

Get ready to discover the essential tools that will make your work more efficient, uncover valuable resources to enhance your skills, and learn the secrets to building a solid foundation for your solopreneur ventures.

Essential Tools for the Solopreneur

1. Productivity Apps:

Invest in tools like **Trello, Asana,** or **Monday.com** to streamline project management. These platforms help you organize tasks, set deadlines, and collaborate seamlessly, enhancing overall productivity.

2. Communication Platforms:

Stay connected with clients and collaborators using communication tools like **Slack** or **Microsoft Teams**. These platforms facilitate efficient communication, file sharing, and team collaboration, essential for a solopreneur juggling multiple roles.

3. Financial Management Software:

Simplify your financial tracking with tools like **QuickBooks** or **FreshBooks**. Efficient financial management is crucial for solopreneurs, helping you monitor expenses, invoice clients, and stay on top of your financial health.

4. Social Media Management:

Leverage social media to amplify your online presence. Tools like **Buffer** or **Hootsuite** allow you to schedule posts, track engagement, and manage multiple social media accounts effortlessly.

5. Website Building Platforms:

Establish your online presence with user-friendly website builders like **Wix** or **Squarespace**. These platforms empower solopreneurs to create professional websites without the need for extensive coding knowledge.

6. Email Marketing Tools:

Nurture client relationships and build your brand with email marketing platforms like **Mailchimp** or **ConvertKit**. These tools assist in creating engaging campaigns, automating emails, and analyzing performance metrics.

Resources for Skill Development

1. Online Courses and Platforms:

Platforms like **Coursera, Udemy,** and **LinkedIn Learning** offer a myriad of courses across diverse topics. Invest time in continuous learning to enhance your skills, whether it's in marketing, graphic design, or business strategy.

2. Industry-Specific Associations:

Joining associations related to your industry provides networking opportunities and access to valuable resources. Stay updated on industry trends and connect with fellow professionals through organizations relevant to your field.

3. Mentorship Programs:

Seek guidance from experienced mentors who can offer insights into your industry. Mentorship programs, both formal and informal, provide a valuable support system and a wealth of knowledge to navigate challenges.

4. Books and Publications:

Expand your knowledge base through literature. Books, industry publications, and business journals are rich sources of information that can offer profound insights and perspectives.

5. Webinars and Workshops:

Attend webinars and workshops hosted by industry experts. These interactive sessions provide real-time learning experiences, allowing you to stay updated on emerging trends and best practices.

Building a Strong Foundation for Sustained Success

1. Clear business vision and goals:

Define your business vision and set clear, achievable goals. A solopreneur's journey thrives on purpose and direction, providing a roadmap for sustained success.

2. Effective Time Management:

Master the art of time management. Prioritize tasks, set deadlines, and allocate time effectively to ensure optimal productivity without burnout.

3. Financial Literacy:

Develop a strong understanding of your finances. Regularly review budgets, track income and expenses, and make informed financial decisions to secure the financial health of your venture.

4. Adaptability and Resilience:

Embrace change and remain adaptable in the face of challenges. Entrepreneurship demands resilience; view setbacks as opportunities for growth and learning.

5. Client Relationship Building:

Cultivate strong client relationships. Communication, reliability, and delivering exceptional value are pillars for sustained success as an entrepreneur.

6. Personal Well-Being:

Prioritize your well-being. A healthy work-life balance, self-care, and occasional breaks contribute to sustained productivity and prevent burnout.

In conclusion, the solopreneurial journey is a dynamic adventure, and equipping yourself with the right tools, continuously enhancing your skills, and building a robust foundation are critical elements for sustained success. As you navigate the intricate landscape of entrepreneurship, remember that your journey is uniquely yours. Embrace the challenges, celebrate the victories, and craft an entrepreneurial narrative that reflects your passion and resilience. Here's to your success as a solopreneur. May your efforts be successful, and may your influence persist.

7

Learning from the Masters

Robert T. Kiyosaki

R obert T. Kiyosaki's voice echoes powerfully in the labyrinth of financial education. His book, Rich Dad, Poor Dad, is truly remarkable, and I highly recommend it. It has the power to inspire and guide individuals on their journey towards creating wealth, offering invaluable insights and wisdom. Kiyosaki embarked on a remarkable path towards financial enlightenment, fueled by a distinct perspective instilled in him by his rich dad. This exceptional mentor's wisdom would go on to profoundly impact Kiyosaki's life. Kiyosaki's teachings are all about questioning conventional beliefs and norms when it comes to money and wealth. This "Rich Dad, Poor Dad" book stands as a powerful testament for individuals in search of a different route to financial success.

In Kiyosaki's teachings, there is a fundamental concept that holds great significance: the clear differentiation between assets and liabilities.

This profound realization has the power to reshape the financial future of numerous individuals and provide a solid understanding of how wealth is generated.

According to Kiyosaki's philosophy, assets play a crucial role in achieving financial success. Assets are not just ordinary possessions; they are powerful entities that generate income for us. The standard examples, such as real estate, stocks, and businesses, exemplify this powerful principle. They have the power to generate income, increase in value, and act as vehicles for developing long-term wealth.

Embracing the concept of assets goes far beyond a mere focus on material possessions. It involves recognizing opportunities that can bring us benefits, help us grow, and enhance our financial well-being.

Kiyosaki's concept inspires us to view assets as powerful tools that drive us towards financial freedom, urging us to prioritize their acquisition and growth.

In contrast, liabilities in Kiyosaki's model are entities that have a negative impact on our finances. In this category, we have more than just debts. It also encompasses all ongoing expenses that don't contribute to building wealth. The family house, often seen as a symbol of success, can become a burden if it uses up more resources than it generates.

This distinction presents an exciting opportunity to challenge the conventional belief that acquiring possessions is the sole measure of financial prosperity. It's important to take a step back and evaluate our choices, especially when it comes to our finances. Let's reflect on whether the things we perceive as assets are truly benefiting our financial well-being.

Kiyosaki's teachings highlight the fundamental distinction in how the wealthy and the less fortunate approach and handle assets and liabilities. Assets have the power to not only generate income for the wealthy but also open doors to acquiring even more assets. It's a cycle of growth and opportunity. It's an incredible journey of growth and progress that drives them towards financial success.

However, it's important to note that the middle class and those facing financial difficulties often struggle with effectively managing their finances, sometimes mistaking liabilities for assets. The family home, with its mortgage debt and maintenance costs, serves as a great example. Kiyosaki's concept encourages a powerful shift in mindset: moving away from acquiring liabilities and instead focusing on actively acquiring assets that generate income.

Kiyosaki's teachings go beyond just acquiring assets; they dive into the strategic use of leverage. When used effectively, leverage can significantly enhance the potential return on investment! Using other people's money (OPM) to invest in real estate or businesses can greatly amplify profits. It's an incredibly powerful strategy that can lead to significant financial gains.

This concept truly challenges the idea that wealth creation is limited to those who are already wealthy. It opens up new possibilities for everyone to create their own wealth, regardless of their starting point. Kiyosaki's philosophy is all about empowering individuals to harness their knowledge, skills, and resources to strategically acquire income-generating assets. This sets off a wonderful cycle of positive feedback that propels financial growth at an accelerated pace.

Kiyosaki's teachings emphasize the importance of cultivating a mindset that leads to wealth and success. It's all about refining your skills to spot opportunities in situations that others might perceive as challenges. Every challenge we face becomes an opportunity for growth, and every setback is a chance to learn and improve. Embracing this mindset shift is crucial for successfully navigating the ever-changing relationship between assets and liabilities.

Throughout the chapter, we share inspiring real-life stories of individuals who have successfully applied Kiyosaki's principles to completely transform their financial landscapes. These narratives showcase the powerful results that come from embracing the asset vs. liability paradigm. From strategic investments in real estate to seizing business opportunities, they demonstrate the tangible impact of this mindset.

Remember that it's important to carefully evaluate our financial portfolio, recognize our true assets, and find ways to reduce liabilities. Embracing a new mindset, being open to continuous learning, and dedicating ourselves to strategic wealth creation are key ingredients for success.

8

The Power of Passive Income

S tep into the realm of financial empowerment, where the knowledge and utilization of passive income streams can lead you towards a future of financial stability and freedom. In this chapter, we will dive into the fascinating world of passive income, uncovering the secrets to building sustainable sources of revenue and mastering the art of striking a perfect balance between active and passive income.

Embracing Passive Income Streams

Passive income is the key to achieving financial independence; it's the income that keeps flowing in with little effort required once you've made your initial investment of time, money, or resources. It offers a refreshing alternative to the typical work routine, enabling you to create financial prosperity while freeing yourself from the limitations of a conventional 9-to-5 job. There are many different forms of passive income streams:

Investments can be a great way to generate passive income. Dividends from stocks, interest from bonds, and rental income from real estate are all examples of how you can make your money work for you. By investing wisely, you can create a steady stream of income that can positively impact your financial future.

If you're an author, musician, or creator, royalties from books, music, or intellectual property can provide a consistent source of passive income.

Real Estate: Owning rental properties or engaging in real estate crowdfunding enables you to generate passive income by benefiting from property appreciation and rental payments.

Online Ventures: Discover the endless possibilities of generating passive income through online platforms. Explore the world of creating and selling digital products, affiliate marketing, and earning from online courses. Embrace the power of the internet to unlock your financial potential.

Understanding the mechanics of passive income is similar to planting seeds today to reap the benefits tomorrow. Making an initial investment of time, resources, or money can result in a consistent flow of income that contributes to long-term financial stability and growth.

Building a solid foundation for long-term financial stability:

1. Make smart investments and ensure that your investment portfolio is well-diversified, including a variety of stocks, bonds, real estate, and other assets. It's important to consistently evaluate and adjust your investments to ensure they are in line with your financial objectives and comfort level with risk.

2. Establish a Strong Online Presence: Harness the potential of the internet to develop digital products, engage in affiliate marketing, or

set up an online business. The online realm is a fantastic platform that allows you to connect with people from all over the world and create reliable sources of passive income.

3. Real Estate Ventures: Think about real estate as a solid asset class for generating passive income. Investing in rental properties, real estate investment trusts (REITs), or crowdfunding platforms can offer a reliable stream of income.

4. Intellectual Property: For all the creators out there, it's time to embrace the exciting possibilities of monetizing your intellectual property. By licensing your work, participating in royalty programs, and selling digital products, you have the opportunity to generate a steady stream of income. This can provide you with a positive and sustainable financial future, help you achieve fluency in your earnings, and motivate you to continue pursuing your creative endeavors.

5. Automation and delegation: Capitalizing on the power of automation is crucial for building a sustainable source of passive income. Utilize tools and systems to streamline processes, and explore the option of delegating tasks to create more space for strategic planning and expansion.

Achieving Financial Stability through a Balanced Income Approach:

Attaining financial stability goes beyond simply maximizing passive income. It involves finding a harmonious balance between active and passive revenue streams. Here's a helpful guide to successfully navigating this delicate balance:

1. Make active income a priority: While it's important to focus on building passive income, don't forget about the value of active income. Your primary income source, whether it's from a job or a business,

serves as the foundation for your investments and ventures.

2. Expanding Income Sources: Having a variety of income streams is crucial for maintaining stability. Having a diverse range of income streams is key to building a strong and secure financial portfolio. When faced with challenges, it's important to remember that there are always other sources that can help compensate and overcome any obstacles.

3. Embrace Growth Opportunities: As your passive income continues to increase, it's worth considering reinvesting a portion of it into new ventures or expanding your existing ones. This can help you further capitalize on your success and continue to build momentum. Take on this continuous process that drives perpetual growth and elevates your financial stability.

4. Building an Emergency Fund: It's important to have a strong emergency fund in place. Having a financial safety net in place can provide a sense of security and peace of mind, especially during times of unexpected expenses or a decrease in active income. It allows for a more comfortable and confident approach to handling financial challenges.

5. Consistently evaluate your financial portfolio to ensure its stability and growth. Assess the progress of your investments, adapt strategies according to market conditions, and ensure that your financial plan is in line with your changing goals.

Mastering the art of balancing active and passive income is like conducting a harmonious financial symphony. It requires careful planning, flexibility, and a deep understanding of your financial situation.

Always keep in mind that financial empowerment is a constantly evolving process. It's all about creating a strong and varied income portfolio that perfectly aligns with your life goals. It is not a quick fix for becoming rich overnight. Instead, it is a methodical and purposeful process that, with time, enables you to liberate yourself from financial limitations. By establishing reliable sources of income and balancing active and passive earnings, you are paving the way towards financial stability, flexibility, and long-term prosperity.

9

Wise Investments

Investing is a powerful tool that, when wielded wisely, can transform money from a passive asset into an active force working for your financial goals. The key is understanding the various avenues available and making informed decisions. Here's a comprehensive chapter on wise investments that can make your money work for you.

1. **Stock Market Investments**: Investing in the stock market is an incredible opportunity to grow your wealth and achieve financial success. Investing in shares of companies allows you to become a part-owner and reap the rewards of their growth and success. By spreading your investments across various sectors, you can reduce risk and maximize your potential returns. It's a smart move that can lead to greater financial success.

2. **Real Estate:** Investing in real estate can be an exciting and rewarding opportunity. Whether it's residential properties, commercial spaces, or real estate investment trusts (REITs), the value of real estate tends to appreciate over time. Furthermore, rental income has the potential to

offer a consistent stream of cash flow.

3. **Retirement accounts,** like 401(k)s or IRAs, provide incredible tax advantages and help you build a secure nest egg for the future. It's a smart move that sets you up for financial success down the road. These accounts offer exciting investment options such as mutual funds, which can help your money grow steadily over time through compound interest.

4. **Bonds:** Bonds are incredible investment opportunities that allow you to support governments or corporations while earning regular interest payments and getting your principal amount back when the bond matures. While considered lower-risk compared to stocks, they offer a more stable investment option.

5. **Mutual funds** are an incredible investment opportunity that allows multiple investors to come together and pool their money. By doing so, they can create a diversified portfolio of stocks, bonds, or other assets. This not only spreads the risk but also opens up a world of possibilities for potential returns. It's a fantastic way to grow your wealth and achieve your financial goals. Even if a person doesn't have a lot of experience in the field, our platform provides a straightforward and convenient way for them to access a variety of investments.

6. **Dividend Stocks:** Investing in dividend-paying stocks can provide you with a consistent stream of income. Investing in companies that pay dividends can be incredibly rewarding. Not only do these companies distribute a portion of their earnings to shareholders, but they also offer a consistent source of cash flow. This can be a great way to supplement your investment returns and potentially see your capital grow over time.

7. **Peer-to-Peer Lending:** Platforms that facilitate peer-to-peer lending provide an incredible opportunity to directly lend money to individuals or small businesses, receiving interest payments in return. Although there may be some risks involved, exploring this opportunity could potentially lead to the generation of passive income.

8. **Cryptocurrencies** such as Bitcoin and Ethereum have become increasingly popular as alternative investments. Although they can be unpredictable, they have the potential to generate significant profits. It's absolutely essential to wholeheartedly embrace the opportunity to thoroughly research and understand the potential risks before taking the plunge into the exciting world of the cryptocurrency market.

9. **Education and skill development** are truly invaluable investments that can often be overlooked. It's important to recognize the immense value in investing in yourself and your personal growth. By continuously learning and developing new skills, you are opening up endless opportunities for personal and professional success. So, don't underestimate the power of education and skill development in shaping your future! Expanding your knowledge and honing your skills can pave the way for greater financial prospects, a wider range of career options, and the potential for entrepreneurial triumph.

10. **Pursuing entrepreneurial ventures:** Embarking on the journey of starting your own business or investing in a startup can be an exciting and potentially rewarding experience. Embarking on a successful entrepreneurial journey can be incredibly rewarding, both personally and financially. It's a chance to explore new opportunities and experience significant growth.

In conclusion, wise investments are not about chasing the hottest trends but rather understanding your financial goals, risk tolerance, and time horizon. Diversification, research, and a long-term perspective are essential components of successful investment strategies. Through making well-informed decisions across a variety of investment options, you can tap into the potential of compounding and witness your money actively striving to build wealth and achieve financial freedom. Remember, the journey of wealth creation begins with a well-informed step into the world of wise investments.

10

How to Succeed

E mbarking on the journey to financial freedom is an exciting adventure, filled with opportunities for growth and success. However, it's important to acknowledge that there may be obstacles along the way. Success in this pursuit requires a mindset that not only embraces the rewards but also confronts and overcomes the hurdles along the way.

Challenges are a part of life, whether they come in the form of financial setbacks, market fluctuations, or unexpected life events. The key lies in viewing challenges not as roadblocks but as opportunities for growth. Develop a proactive mindset, seek solutions, and learn from setbacks. Always keep in mind that the road to financial freedom is a continuous journey, where every obstacle you encounter serves as a valuable opportunity to move closer to your aspirations.

Achieving financial freedom often requires a positive mindset and a willingness to step outside of your comfort zone. It's important to take calculated risks along the way, as they can lead to great rewards. Whether it's investing in new ventures, exploring innovative opportunities, or strategically allocating resources, taking well-thought-out risks can propel you forward. Make sure you do your homework well, consider the possible consequences, and don't hesitate to take risks. It is often through taking calculated risks that extraordinary achievements come to fruition.

Resilience and adaptability form the foundation for achieving financial freedom. Having the resilience to overcome obstacles, adapt when needed, and confidently navigate through unknowns is truly priceless. Cultivate resilience by viewing challenges as temporary road bumps rather than insurmountable obstacles. Adaptability is also important; the financial world is changing, and being flexible in your approach helps you prosper in the face of change.

In conclusion, success on the journey to financial freedom is not just about the destination; it's about the resilience you build, the calculated risks you take, and the challenges you overcome. Embrace setbacks as opportunities for growth, venture into calculated risks with unwavering confidence, and let resilience be your guiding force. Always keep in mind that the journey to financial freedom is an exciting and ever-changing experience. It's a path where you overcome challenges, take calculated risks, and embrace adaptability to achieve long-term success. As you embark on this journey, may the pursuit of financial freedom be more than just a goal. Let it be a transformative path that molds your mindset, sharpens your skills, and ultimately guides you towards a life of abundance and fulfillment.

11

The Rules of the Mind

I n this chapter, let's take a moment to revisit some fundamental rules that are often overlooked or simply go unnoticed—those governing the powerhouse of our existence, our mind. Our mind, which is a powerful ally, functions according to simple principles that, when utilized to their full potential, have the potential to significantly simplify our lives. It is the thing that will allow us to bring our dreams into reality, satisfy our desires, and achieve the success that we so desperately seek. In order to live a life that is more satisfying and successful, let us dissect the simplicity that lies within these rules and give ourselves the ability to unleash the true potential that lies within our minds.

Here's how the mind works:

The mind learns by repetition:

Our minds are wired to learn through repetition. When you consistently affirm positive statements, such as "I am confident and capable," you reinforce these beliefs in your subconscious mind. Repetition creates new neural pathways, rewiring your thoughts to align with your desired outcomes. Imagine learning a new language. Consistent daily practice reinforces vocabulary and grammar, creating neural pathways for fluent communication over time. Practice daily affirmations to instill empowering beliefs and amplify your self-confidence.

The mind cannot hold conflicting beliefs or thoughts:

Conflicting beliefs create internal resistance and can hinder your progress. For instance, if you believe "I am not good enough" while also aspiring for success, these conflicting thoughts will cancel each other out. To overcome this, identify and challenge limiting beliefs. If you strive for a healthier lifestyle but hold the belief that you dislike exercise, these conflicting thoughts may hinder progress. Aligning your thoughts with the belief that exercise brings joy can harmonize your mindset and support your health goals. Replace them with empowering beliefs, like "I am worthy of success," to create harmony and alignment within your mind.

Imagination is more powerful than knowledge:

Albert Einstein once said, "Imagination is everything. It is a preview of life's coming attractions." Your imagination has the power to shape your reality. Visualize yourself confidently achieving your goals, and your mind will begin to work towards turning those visions into tangible results. When envisioning a successful presentation, your mind starts laying the groundwork for achievement. Imagination fuels confidence, providing a mental blueprint for success that transcends mere knowledge. Embrace the power of positive visualization to attract success into your life.

Your mind always does what it thinks you want it to do:

Your mind responds to the messages you send consistently. If you frequently express determination and focus on your goals, your mind will work diligently to seek opportunities that align with your aspirations. Consistently expressing determination to achieve career goals signals your mind to actively seek opportunities. Clear communication with your mind through intentional thoughts influences its actions in alignment with your aspirations. Be intentional with your thoughts and communicate clearly to your mind what you desire to achieve.

Your mind works to move you from pain to pleasure:

The mind is programmed to seek pleasure and avoid pain. Use this rule to your advantage by associating pleasure with positive behaviors and outcomes. For example, when facing challenging tasks, visualize the sense of accomplishment and joy that await you upon completion. Linking the pleasure of personal growth to challenging tasks shifts your perspective. Visualizing the joy of overcoming obstacles transforms the mind's perception, motivating you to embrace challenges fearlessly. By linking pleasure to growth and success, you motivate your mind to embrace new opportunities fearlessly.

Your mind responds to the pictures and words you install:

The images and words you choose to focus on shape your reality. When you consistently use empowering affirmations like "I am capable and resilient," you reinforce positive thought patterns and build self-confidence. Affirmations like "I am capable and resilient" install positive thought patterns. By visualizing success and consistently focusing on empowering words, you shape a mindset that fuels self-confidence and accomplishment. Install powerful images of your desired outcomes in your mind, and your subconscious will work tirelessly to manifest them

Your mind wants to stay with what is familiar while avoiding what is unfamiliar:

Stepping out of your comfort zone can be challenging, as the mind prefers familiarity. However, personal growth requires embracing new experiences and breaking free from limitations. Challenge yourself regularly to expand your horizons and adopt a growth mindset. Stepping out of your comfort zone, like trying a new hobby, challenges the mind's preference for familiarity. Embracing unfamiliar experiences fosters personal growth and expands your mental landscape. As you stretch your boundaries, your mind will adapt and evolve, opening new doors of opportunity.

Whatever you focus on, you get more of it:

The mind is a powerful magnet that attracts experiences and opportunities based on your focus. Direct your attention towards your goals and aspirations. Concentrating on career goals and visualizing success magnetizes your mind to opportunities aligned with your aspirations. Focusing on positivity attracts more positive experiences into your life. By maintaining a positive outlook and focusing on the positive aspects of your journey, you'll attract opportunities and experiences aligned with your desires.

You make your beliefs, and then your beliefs make you:

Your beliefs serve as the foundation of your actions and outcomes. Choose empowering beliefs that support your growth and success.

45

Choosing beliefs that align with your potential and possibilities sets the stage for growth. Believing in your capabilities forms the foundation for actions that lead to success. When you believe in your abilities and possibilities, you create fertile ground for your dreams to flourish.

Your thoughts form a blueprint that your mind and body work to make your reality:

Thoughts act as blueprints, influencing your actions and emotions. Nourish positive thoughts to create a blueprint for success and happiness. Consistent positive visualization creates a mental blueprint for success. Your mind and body collaborate to turn these visions into tangible reality through aligned actions. When you consistently visualize your desired outcomes and maintain a positive mindset, your mind and body work in harmony to manifest these visions into your reality.

Your mind does not know the difference between good or bad, true or false, healthy or unhealthy, right or wrong; it simply acts on your words regardless:

The mind operates on the information it receives without discerning its truth or accuracy. Therefore, be mindful of the words you use, both in self-talk and when communicating with others. Using constructive language when facing challenges influences your mind to respond positively. Mindful communication shapes your mental environment and guides your actions towards positive outcomes. Simply use constructive and empowering language to guide your mind towards positive outcomes.

Every thought you have causes a physical reaction and an emo-

tional response:

Thoughts trigger physiological and emotional responses in your body. Positive thoughts elevate your mood and create a sense of well-being, while negative thoughts can lead to stress and tension. Positive thoughts trigger feelings of happiness and well-being, promoting emotional balance. On the contrary, negative thoughts may lead to stress and tension, highlighting the mind-body connection and the importance of maintaining a positive mental space. Practice mindfulness and cultivate awareness of your thoughts to maintain emotional balance and overall well-being.

As we wrap up, I invite you to not just understand but to actively implement these simple rules of the mind. By putting them into practice, you open the door to limitless possibilities, transform dreams into reality, and pave the way for your own undeniable success.

12

Conclusion

Unleashing Your Financial Potential

F inancial freedom is a multifaceted concept that goes beyond mere wealth accumulation. It involves gaining control over one's financial destiny, making choices aligned with personal values, and contributing positively to one's own life and the lives of others. Financial freedom provides the means to pursue dreams, achieve personal and professional growth, and live a fulfilling and purposeful life.

The different aspects of financial freedom include defining financial goals, overcoming mental barriers, exploring online income opportunities, understanding mindset versus action, and going deeper into the concepts of assets and liabilities. Don't forget to adopt a mindset that prioritizes growth, resilience, and adaptability.

The importance of passive income and how it can contribute to long-term financial stability.

By adding different passive income streams, such as real estate, intellectual property, and online ventures,. emphasizes the need to balance active and passive income for overall financial stability.

Setbacks and challenges are inevitable on the path to financial freedom. Simply view challenges as opportunities for growth, take calculated risks, and develop resilience and adaptability.

Roughly, set personalized goals, overcome mental barriers, explore online opportunities, understand the power of mindset, and strive for a balance between active and passive income to achieve lasting financial freedom.

Congratulations on taking this first step! Reading through this book is truly admirable and deserves a round of applause. Consider this your own exciting journey, where challenges are hidden opportunities, setbacks are building blocks, and every moment is an opportunity for personal growth. Remember that true value is found not only in reaching your destination but also in embracing the enriching journey of transformation.

You have the ability to shape your financial future, break free from limitations, and live the life you have always desired. Accept the power of wisdom, question your beliefs, and let resilience be your guide. Now is the perfect moment to show off your talents, envision extraordinary achievements, set ambitious goals, and cultivate a life filled with prosperity. Prepare yourself to uncover your hidden abilities and release the remarkable. You have the power to overcome any challenge that lies ahead; believe in yourself and keep pushing forward!

Your Action Steps

Now that you have gained insights and wisdom, let us put them into action. It is time to take your first flight and take the following steps to shape your own path to financial freedom.

1. Set Your Personalized Goals: Define what financial freedom means to you. Whether it's owning a home, traveling the world, or early retirement, let your goals reflect your dreams and values. Be specific about what you want and when you want it.
2. Take strategic steps: Break down your goals into manageable steps. Just like building an emergency fund, celebrate small wins on your journey. For long-term goals, such as retirement, engage in strategic planning and consistent effort.
3. Challenge Your Mindset: Embrace the 80% mindset, 20% action principle. Your thoughts and beliefs are powerful. Focus on growth and positivist, knowing that the right mindset contributes significantly to success.
4. Diversify Your Income: Explore online opportunities, from free-lancing to online businesses. Align your passion with market needs. The digital world offers endless possibilities—seize them.
5. Invest in Knowledge: Continuous learning is key. Explore courses, webinars, and networking events to stay ahead in your chosen field. Knowledge is your currency for success.
6. Implement Passive Income Strategies: Explore avenues for passive income, such as real estate, online ventures, and intellectual property. Plant seeds today for a harvest of financial stability

tomorrow.

Remember that this is more than just a book; it is a transformative experience. I know it was a lot to assimilate; let it sink in, but don't wait too long. Your action today paves the way for the financial independence you deserve. Grab these opportunities, and let your dream life begin!

If you have found this book to be beneficial, I would greatly appreciate it if you could kindly leave a positive review.

Rise and Soar,

Isabelle

Set Yourself to Soaring Success

My Amazing Life-Changing Program

"Entrepreneurs, Revolutionize Your Mindset, Rise and Thrive: From Limitations to Soaring success"

"Unlock the path to mastery in your entrepreneurial journey. Engage in my dynamic 4-week program tailored to help you overcome limitations, develop resilience, and attain sustainable success. Embrace the tools and mindset needed to rise above challenges and reach new heights of achievement."

Are you an entrepreneur stuck in a loop of limitations and old patterns that prevent you from achieving the success you desire?

Do you struggle to find clarity and consistency on your path to greatness?

Well, the time for change has arrived. Introducing the Success Elevator Program, your ticket to unblocking yourself, obtaining unshakable self-confidence, and reaching soaring success.

You may be asking, "What exactly does this program offer?"

It's simple. My 1-month program is specifically designed to release your old limiting patterns and install positive mind programming. Imagine breaking free from the chains that have been holding you back, allowing you to achieve the success you've always dreamt of.

Why do you need the Success Elevator Program? I understand the pain and frustration you're experiencing. My program is your solution, providing you with the tools and strategies to overcome your limitations, gain clarity, and develop consistency in your entrepreneurial journey.

I know your time is precious, so this program allows you to quickly and permanently release what is no longer serving you. I effectively guide you to dive to the root cause of what is holding you back from soaring success.

Don't settle for a life of mediocrity and frustration. My Success Elevator Program is your ticket to rewriting your success story. Imagine unblocking yourself, gaining clarity, and achieving unshakable self-confidence.

This program is your opportunity to leave old patterns behind and soar to new heights of success.

Join the Success Elevator Program today and unlock your limitless potential.

Say goodbye to limitations, embrace consistency, and experience the fulfillment of reaching your highest aspirations.

Ready to soar?

Join now:

www.isabelleboily.com/Soar

About the Author

Get ready to meet Isabelle Boily, the driving force behind the Success Elevator Movement, a beacon of inspiration crafted specifically for solo, future, or established entrepreneurs and the rebels who embrace their "black sheep" status. Isabelle's life plays out like a blockbuster, characterized by resiliency, innovation, and an unwavering passion to assist ambitious people facing scarcity to break free and redefine success on their terms.

Isabelle's journey spans a diverse landscape: festivals, military camps in Bosnia, managing a Caribbean landscaping company, cruising U.S. roads in a semi truck, and orchestrating a bed and breakfast in Brittany. In 2017, she faced a plot twist that brought her back to Quebec, settling in a secluded cabin surrounded by nature. Here, she embarked on a journey of self-discovery, creating a life that thrives on abundance despite scarcity's looming shadows.

Isabelle's program, "S.E.T. Yourself for Success," is a unique narrative that echoes the heartbeat of her audience:

Creating Meaningful Moments: Isabelle gets the solo hustle, emphasizing quality time for those navigating entrepreneurial terrain.

Monetizing Personal Gifts: Guiding rebels to turn their unique gifts into financial freedom, Isabelle unlocks the potential hidden within each entrepreneur.

Working Anywhere in the World: Advocating for a work style that transcends borders, Success Elevator resonates with the nomadic spirit of her ambitious audience.

Adopting Healthy Habits: Recognizing the challenges of a demanding lifestyle, Isabelle champions the physical and mental well-being of her solo trailblazers.

Giving Back: Isabelle champions the underdogs, empowering solo entrepreneurs and offering a helping hand to those considered the "black sheep" in their pursuits.

Isabelle Boily, a change specialist, holds a unique lantern, guiding solo entrepreneurs through significant life changes. Her career story spans various countries, reflecting her ease in embracing both subtle and radical transformations—an anthem for the unconventional.

Certified in massage therapy, Reiki, Emotional Code, and Rapid Transformational Therapy, Isabelle faced her share of challenges, inspiring the birth of Success Elevator in 2019—a lifeline for solo entrepreneurs aiming to overcome scarcity and achieve abundance.

Isabelle's diverse background includes chapters as a former party animal, ex-bed and breakfast owner in Europe, dog enthusiast, photography buff, Caribbean landscaping manager, sailboat assistant captain, communication expert in Bosnia, resilient and independent, divorced, massage therapist, emotion code practitioner, and rapid transformation therapy practitioner.

In Isabelle's world, the law of attraction rules, dreams manifest, birds sing in harmony, and homes transform under her skilled hands. Isabelle, a daily meditator, took the plunge and authored her first affirmations book in 2023.

Join Isabelle on the Success Elevator journey—a masterclass in resilience, delivered with a touch of humor and a commitment to transforming the lives of entrepreneurs and the black sheep who dare to dream.

You can connect with me on:

🌐 https://www.isabelleboily.com

📘 https://www.facebook.com/IsabelleBoily.Success

🔗 https://www.youtube.com/@IsabelleBoilySuccessElevator

🔗 https://www.instagram.com/successelevatortherapy

Subscribe to my newsletter:

✉️   https://mailchi.mp/isabelleboily.com/success-elevator-newsletter

Also by Isabelle Boily

Affirmation Made Easy: Your Practical Guide to a positive Mindset
Discover the power of affirmations and how they can transform your life. This straightforward guide covers 3200 affirmations organized by chakras, covering topics like health, wealth, love, job, anxiety, grief, self-confidence, and more. Plus, you'll learn how to write your own affirmations.